# Mighty
# TRAINS

### Chris Oxlade

W

An Appleseed Editions book

First published in 2006 by Franklin Watts

Paperback edition 2008

Franklin Watts
338 Euston Road, London NW1 3BH

Franklin Watts Australia
Level 17/207 Kent St, Sydney, NSW 2000

© 2006 Appleseed Editions

Appleseed Editions Ltd
Well House, Friars Hill, Guestling, East Sussex TN35 4ET

Created by Q2A Creative
Editor: Chester Fisher
Designers: Amandeep K. Bakshi, Ashita Murgai
Picture Researchers: Lalit Dalal, Somnath Bowmick

ISBN 978 0 7496 7591 2

Dewey Classification: 625.1

A CIP catalogue for this book is available from the British Library.

Picture credits
t=top b=bottom c=centre l=left r=right
Albert Jeans: 14b, Alstom: 16 & 17t, Bridgnorth cliff railway: 25t, Chris Barton: 5b,
Ffestiniog Railway Co: 13b, Gregor.V/www.Parovoz.com: 9b, Hashimoto Noboru/Corbis Sygma: 29t,
Jeff Williams/Shutterstock: 8b, Orient-Express Hotels, Trains & Cruises: 20c & 20br & 21b,
Pilatus-Bahnen: 24, Rail Photo Library: 15tr & 18b & 19t & 23b & 27t & 27b,
Rebecca Picard/Shutterstock: 5t, Science and Society Picture Library: 10t & 10-11cb,
Siemens AG: 4b, 6b, 7t, 9cl, 14t, 17b, 22cr, 22b & 26b,
Shutterstock: 12b & 13t, Steamtown National Historic Site: 23t
The Trans-Siberian Express Company/GW Travel Ltd: 21t
www.steamlocomotive.com: 11t & 31tr

Printed in Singapore

Franklin Watts is a division of Hachette Children's Books

# CONTENTS

# MIGHTY TRAINS

**Every day thousands of trains carry millions of passengers and millions of tonnes of freight between towns and cities all over the world.**

## TYPES OF TRAINS

There are two main types of train: passenger trains and freight trains. Passenger trains come in several different forms. High-speed trains operate non-stop between big cities. Commuter trains carry workers into cities and out again. Light-rail trains (or trams) run through city centres. All trains are made up of two or more rail vehicles linked together.

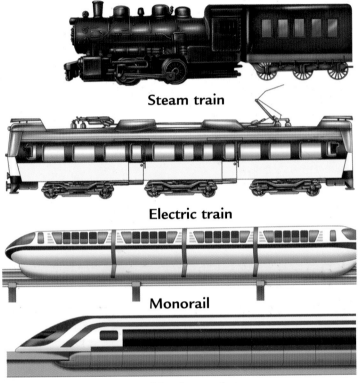

Steam train

Electric train

Monorail

Maglev train

The ICE 3 is a high-speed train that carries passengers in great comfort at speeds over 300 kph (186 mph).

# TRACK AND INFRASTRUCTURE

Trains would be useless without tracks to travel on. Most tracks are made up of two metal rails supported on concrete or wooden sleepers. The distance between the rails is called the track gauge. Railways also need other infrastructure such as stations, bridges and tunnels, as well as signals to control the trains.

A busy train station where many people arrive and depart.

## FAST FACTS

**Busiest Station**
The world's busiest station is Shinjuku Station in Tokyo, Japan. It sees some 1.6 million passengers pass through daily.

Railway track stretching into the Bolivian desert. There are millions of kilometres of railway track in the world.

# ELECTRIC TRAINS

**The wheels of an electric locomotive are turned by electric motors. Electric locomotives are fast, quiet and clean.**

## ELECTRIC LOCOMOTIVES

A locomotive is a railway vehicle that pulls other vehicles, such as passenger carriages or freight wagons. An electric locomotive picks up electricity from an overhead cable. Electrical machinery in the locomotive changes the voltage of the electricity and controls how it flows to the electric traction motors that turn the wheels.

## Transformer and rectifier
**Reduces voltage and changes to direct current**

## Pantograph
**Collects high-voltage alternating current**

### Siemens 1047 Eurosprinter

| | |
|---|---|
| Power | 8,582 horsepower |
| Weight | 86 tonnes |
| Traction motors | 2 |
| Top speed | 230 kph (143 mph) |

*A modern electric locomotive that pulls freight wagons in Europe.*

## Bogie
**Contains wheels and traction motors**

ES 64 F4 - 001

SIEMENS

www.dispolok.com

In an electric multiple unit (EMU), each carriage has its own traction motors. There is no separate locomotive.

# BOGIES

All modern trains have bogies. A bogie is a frame with four (or sometimes six) wheels. A locomotive has two bogies, one at each end. The bogies swivel from side to side when the locomotive goes round a bend on the track. A locomotive bogie has a traction motor that turns its wheels.

## FAST FACTS
**The Third Rail**
*Some electric locomotives get their electricity from an extra rail in the track called the third rail.*

Traction motor

Bogie frame

Wheel

The bogie system on the Paris Metro.

7

# DIESEL TRAINS

**The power that moves a diesel train comes from a giant on-board diesel engine. Diesel locomotives can travel where there is no electricity supply.**

## DIESEL LOCOMOTIVE

Most diesel locomotives are actually diesel-electric locomotives. This means that the diesel engine turns an electricity generator. The generator makes electricity that works electric traction motors that turn the wheels. Some diesel locomotives are diesel-mechanical locomotives, which means the diesel engine drives the wheels by gears. Diesel hydraulics are driven by hydraulic systems.

### Locomotive number
Identifies the locomotive

### Running light
This is white when train is moving forwards at night.

**General Electric Genesis**

| | |
|---|---|
| Power | 4,200 horsepower |
| Weight | 121 tonnes |
| Traction motors | 4 |
| Top speed | 177 kph (110 mph) |

A giant diesel-electric locomotive used to pull passenger trains in the USA.

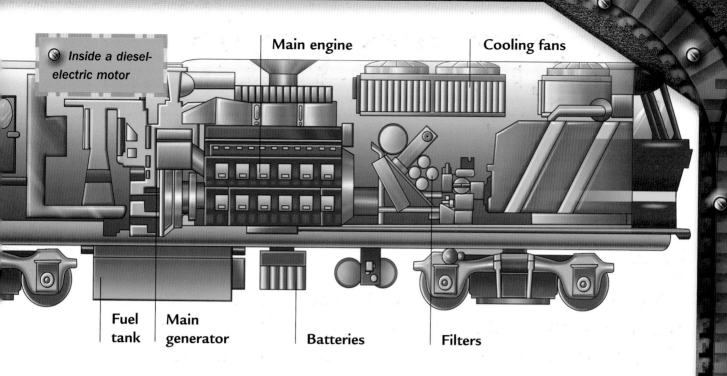

Inside a diesel-electric motor

**Main engine**

**Cooling fans**

**Fuel tank**  **Main generator**  **Batteries**  **Filters**

# DIESEL POWER

The diesel engines in diesel locomotives are giant machines. The biggest weigh more than 20 tonnes, and have 16 cylinders and a turbocharger. Each cylinder has a capacity of over 10 litres. A typical car engine with four cylinders only has a total capacity of about 1.6 litres.

## FAST FACTS
**Power Engine**
*The diesel engine from a diesel-electric locomotive is over fifty times more powerful than a typical car engine.*

The controls and instruments in the cab of a diesel locomotive.

# EARLY TRAINS

**The first trains worked in mines more than 250 years ago. They were small trucks pulled by people or horses. Steam locomotives were invented about 200 years ago.**

*Stephenson's Rocket could pull a train at a top speed of 48 kph (30 mph).*

*A 1830s first-class railway carriage was luxurious, but the ride was very bumpy!*

## ROCKET POWER

The *Rocket* is one of the most famous steam locomotives. It was built by the English engineer and inventor, George Stephenson. It won a competition in 1830 to pull trains on one of the first railways, between Liverpool and Manchester in England. Most of the locomotives built later were based on the *Rocket*.

### Buffer
**Stops carriages bumping together as train slows down**

> This is a replica of an American locomotive of the 1860s. At the front is a pilot (or cowcatcher), which protected the locomotive from objects on the track.

Cowcatcher

Cylinder and piston

Driving wheels

Boiler

# IMPROVING POWER AND SPEED

During the 1840s and 1850s, engineers built locomotives with bigger and bigger fireboxes and boilers, which gave more steam at higher pressure. This made the locomotives more powerful. The number of wheels driven by the pistons was increased to four or six. This stopped the wheels slipping.

## FAST FACTS
**Travelling in Comfort**
*On early railways, wealthy passengers could load their horse-drawn carriages onto railway wagons and travel inside them in comfort.*

11

# STEAM TRAINS

**Steam locomotives ruled the railways in the first half of the twentieth century. More efficient and cleaner electric and diesel locomotives took over from them in the 1960s.**

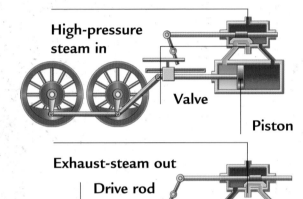

High-pressure steam in

Valve

Piston

Exhaust-steam out

Drive rod

Cylinder

### How it works

A valve lets high–pressure steam into the cylinder to push the piston and drive the wheels. The valve then lets out the exhaust steam.

## STEAM POWER

The energy for a steam locomotive comes from burning coal in the firebox. The hot gases boil water to make high-pressure steam. The steam is piped to the cylinders, where it makes the pistons move in and out, making the wheels turn. A roaring, puffing steam locomotive made an impressive sight as it hurtled along the track.

An 1899 locomotive used in the American West.

A steam locomotive had many dials and valves for the control of steam pressure.

# STEAM TODAY

There are hundreds of steam locomotives still working around the world today. In some countries, such as China and India, steam locomotives still pull passenger and freight trains. There are also many preserved steam locomotives that are run by enthusiasts. They pull passenger trains on scenic railway lines.

## FAST FACTS

**Fastest Steam Train**
*The fastest steam locomotive of all time was a British machine called Mallard. In 1938 it set a speed record of 203 kph (127 mph).*

A preserved steam engine on the Ffestiniog railway in Wales. Originally this railway moved slate from mines to ships at the coast.

PORTHMADOG

No

13

## Saddle tank
**The water tank sits over the firebox**

# HIGH-SPEED

Modern high-speed trains carry passengers quickly and comfortably between cities. These trains can run at over 300 kph (186 mph) on specially built high-speed tracks.

## HIGH-SPEED SETS

All high-speed trains come in train 'sets'. Each set is made up of two streamlined end cars with high-speed carriages in between. The two end cars are normally power cars that collect electricity from overhead cables and send it to the traction motors. Nearly all high-speed trains are powered by electricity.

Inside a carriage of the Spanish Velaro high-speed train.

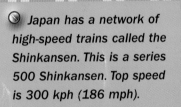
Japan has a network of high-speed trains called the Shinkansen. This is a series 500 Shinkansen. Top speed is 300 kph (186 mph).

**Shinkansen series 500**

| | |
|---|---|
| Power | 24,745 hp |
| Weight | 640 tonnes |
| Number of motors | 64 |
| Top speed | 300 kph (186 mph) |

A Pendolino high-speed train running on a main line in the UK.

Car body tilt angle

Tilting trains are used to overcome problems on curving railway tracks.

Bogie frame

Tilting ram

Track

# TILTING TRAINS

Some high-speed trains tilt over as they go round bends, just as you lean sideways as you go round a corner on a bicycle. Tilting lets the train go faster round the bends than normal because it stops passengers, luggage, cups and other objects flying sideways. The tilting is controlled by on-board computers.

## FAST FACTS
**Fastest Electric Train**
*The fastest speed ever reached by an electric train is 515.3 kph (322 mph), by a TGV train in France in 1990.*

15

# MASS-TRANSIT

**Metro trains and light-rail trains stop at stations in cities. They are designed to transport hundreds of people and are called mass-transit trains.**

## METRO TRAINS

Metro trains are mass-transit trains that run on normal railway tracks. Metro trains have good acceleration so they can get between stations quickly. They are normally electric multiple units or diesel multiple units. Many major cities have underground metros that run through tunnels under the streets.

This is Metro System Shanghai Pearl Line in Shanghai, China.

### Motor car
**Two motor cars are needed for a six-car train**

## Standing room
**Allows lots of passengers to fit into the carriages**

## Sliding doors
**Plenty of doors so passengers can get on and off easily**

A Citidas light-rail train running through the streets of Bordeaux in France.

## FAST FACTS
**First Underground**
*The first underground railway was opened in London in 1863. Trains were pulled by steam locomotives that filled the tunnels with sulphurous fumes.*

# LIGHT RAIL

Trains that run along city streets are called light-rail trains. The trains are lighter than main-line trains, which means the rails do not have to be as strong. Light-rail trains are also called trams. Light-rail trains often share roads with city traffic, but normally have right of way.

Double-decker trains carry more people than single deckers. The floors are linked by stairs.

80-33 022-9

# FREIGHT TRAINS

**Thousands of different pieces of freight, from logs to light bulbs, are carried around the world by huge freight trains. Freight is carried in specialised wagons.**

General freight wagon

Oil container

## CARS, HOPPERS AND TANKERS

There are dozens of different types of freight wagon. The simplest are box cars and flat wagons that can be packed with all sorts of freight. Some flat wagons carry standard metal containers that are also carried by trucks and ships. The different wagons are called rolling stock.

## Flat wagon
**Can carry goods of all shapes and sizes**

◎ *Wagons can be adapted for special uses such as cable laying.*

Containers are put on flat wagons directly from ships.

**Flat wagon**

## Containers
These are standard sizes to fit most wagons

# MULTI HEADERS

A long freight train, with hundreds of wagons, can weigh so much that a single locomotive cannot pull it. So, two, three or even four locomotives are coupled to each other. These trains are called multiple headers. These are often used in mountain regions where there are long, steep sections of track.

A multiple header hauling freight through the Canadian mountains.

MIGHTY TRAINS

# FAMOUS TRAINS

**Some trains are famous for their luxury carriages or for the journeys they take passengers on.**

Carriages of the Orient Express were purpose-built by the Compagnie Internationale des Wagons-Lits.

## LUXURY CARRIAGES

The most famous train of all was the Orient Express. It was the most luxurious way to travel across Europe between the 1880s and the 1940s. The carriages featured leather armchairs, fine carpets and gold decorations. The compartments were sitting rooms by day and then converted to bedrooms at night. Delicious food was served in the dining car.

Inside a restored carriage of the modern-day Orient Express.

# THE LONGEST JOURNEY

The most famous train journey in the world is the Trans-Siberian Express. The train runs from Moscow, all across Russia to Vladivostok on the east coast, about 9,245 kilometres (5,778 miles) away. The trip takes nine or ten days, and the train stops at 91 stations on the way.

The Trans-Siberian Express running through the Russian countryside.

Celebrating 100 years of the Trans-Siberian Express.

## FAST FACTS

**Orient Express**

*The original carriages of the Orient Express have been restored and form a tourist train that is also called the Orient Express.*

MIGHTY TRAINS

TRANS-SIBERIAN EXPRESS
100 Years – 100 Лет
ТРАНС-СИГИРСКИЙ ЭКСПРЕСС
П36          003

# RECORD BREAKERS

On these pages you can find out about some of the world's fastest, longest and biggest trains. They are all record breakers.

## THE FASTEST

Velaro high-speed electric trains run on a purpose-built track between Madrid and Barcelona in Spain. They are designed to run at a top speed of 350 kph (219 mph). This will make them the fastest regular train services in the world. A French TGV train holds the world record for an electric train – of 515 kph (322 mph).

| Velaro high-speed train set | |
|---|---|
| Power | 11,964 hp |
| Weight | 425 tonnes |
| Number of motors | 16 |
| Top speed | 350 kph (217 mph) |
| Number of seats | 404 |

**Driver's cabin**
Spacious and easy to drive

**Nose compartment**
With a coupling mechanism

SIEMENS

The streamlined nose of a Spanish Velaro high-speed train.

*The biggest steam locomotives ever built were the Union Pacific Big Boys of the 1940s. One weighed a massive 549 tonnes.*

## Piston
**Powers four of the sixteen driving wheels**

# FREIGHT MONSTERS

The heaviest and longest trains are mine trains that carry iron ore or coal. They are made up of hundreds of wagons coupled together, with giant diesel locomotives at each end. The heaviest train ever was an Australian ore train assembled in 2001. It featured eight locomotives and 682 wagons, and was 7 kilometres (4 miles) long and weighed 99,732 tonnes.

## FAST FACTS
**The Big Boy**

*Big Boy locomotives had four pistons that turned 16 huge driving wheels. They were 40 metres long.*

MIGHTY TRAINS

*A mammoth Southern Pacific coal train at Tennessee Pass, Colorado USA.*

# MOUNTAIN TRAINS

**Normal trains cannot go up steep hills because their wheels slip on the track. Mountain railways have an extra rail that the trains grip onto with a toothed wheel.**

## THE STEEPEST RAILWAY

On a rack-and-pinion railway the train has a cog or pinion (a toothed wheel) that grips onto a rack (a toothed rail) in the centre of the track. The cog is turned by the train's engine. The steepest rack railway is the Pilatus Railway in Switzerland. In places the track rises up the mountainside at an incredible 48 degrees.

*A train on the Pilatus Railway. The railway gains 1,629 metres in 5 kilometres (3 miles).*

### Stepped carriage
Carriage floor has different levels

### Overhead cables
Supply electricity to train's motors

## Cable
**Pulls carriage up and lowers it down**

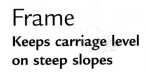
⊘ *One of the trains on a funicular railway in Bridgenorth, UK. It carries passengers up and down a steep hill in the town.*

## Frame
**Keeps carriage level on steep slopes**

# FUNICULAR RAILWAYS

Some mountain railways have a different traction system from the rack-and-pinion system. They are pulled up the mountainside by cables. This sort of system is called a funicular. There are normally two tracks and two trains. As one train goes up the other comes down, so they balance each other.

## FAST FACTS
**Jungfraubahn Railway**
*The Jungfraubahn mountain railway in Switzerland climbs to the top of the Jungfrau mountain. On the way it climbs through a tunnel high inside the famous Eiger mountain.*

**25**

# MONORAIL

A monorail is a railway with one rail instead of the usual two. Monorail trains sit on top of the track or hang underneath it. The tracks are normally supported high in the air.

## STRADDLE MONORAILS

On a straddle monorail the train straddles the rail. The rail is a narrow beam. The train sits on top of the beam and its sides hang down on each side of the beam. The track is normally held in the air on thin concrete columns. This means the track takes up hardly any space on the ground underneath so a monrail can be built over roads and car-parks.

*The Newark International Airport monorail. The trains are powered by electric motors. They run on the track on rubber tyres.*

## Carriages
These have rubber tyres which give traction and stability

**Newark International Airport monorail**

| | |
|---|---|
| Length | 5 km (3 miles) |
| Number of stations | 8 |
| Average speed | 19 kph (12 mph) |
| Opened | 1995 |

## Double track
Made of steel beams and supported on steel columns

## Monorail train
Moved along by electric motors

# SUSPENDED MONORAILS

In some monorail systems, the carriages hang underneath the rail instead of sitting on top of it. In one type of suspended monorail, the wheels run in a channel on top of the rail. Curved arms support the carriages below. In other types, the train's wheels run along the flanges of the beam that form the track. The flange is like a shelf that runs along the beam.

The suspended monorail in Wuppertal, Germany. The trains run above a river most of the time.

## Bogies
With wheels that roll along the top of the rail

## Guide wheels
Roll along each side of the track and steer the train along the track

The Osaka monorail in Japan. The trains roll along the top of concrete beams. There are guide wheels on each side of the beam.

FAST FACTS
**First Monorail**
*The first passenger monorail opened in England in 1825. The train was pulled by a horse that walked along the ground.*

27

# MAGLEV TRAINS

**Maglev is short for magnetic levitation. Maglev trains are the fastest trains of all. In the future, maglevs could travel as fast as jet airliners.**

## MAGNETIC LEVITATION

Maglev trains have no wheels. They are suspended a few centimetres above the track by electromagnets. This means there is no friction between the train and the track, allowing the train to travel at very high speed. Magnets also power the train. There are several working maglev railways around the world.

| Shanghai Transrapid maglev | |
|---|---|
| Track length | 30 km (19 miles) |
| Journey time | 8 minutes |
| Top speed | 430 kph (269 mph) |
| Opened | 2004 |

A Transrapid maglev train. Magnets in the track can be turned on and off to pull the train along the track.

**Nose**
Aerodynamic shape allows train to move smoothly at high speed

An experimental superconducting maglev train running on the Yamanashi Maglev Test Line in Japan.

# SUPERCONDUCTING RAILWAY

The fastest trains in the world run on an experimental maglev railway in Japan. They have reached speeds of more than 580 kph (363 mph). The levitation electromagnets on the train are made of superconducting material, which must be kept extremely cold to work. The track contains propulsion electromagnets along its whole length, making it extremely expensive to build.

A front view of a Transrapid maglev train. This is a monorail maglev.

### Track magnets
**Produce a changing magnetic field**

### On-board magnets
**Attracted by the track magnets**

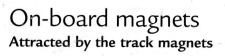

# TIMELINE

## 1769
In France Nicolas Cugnot builds a steam carriage, the first steam-powered vehicle.

## 1774
Scotsman James Watt builds a steam engine.

## 1789
In England, William Jessup invents the flanged wheel to keep railways wagons on a track.

## 1804
Englishman Richard Trevithick builds one of the first-ever steam locomotives.

## 1825
George Stephenson completes his steam locomotive, which pulls trains on the Stockton & Darlington Railway in England.

## 1830
The *Best Friend* is the first steam locomotive built in the USA. It works on the Charlston & Hamburg railroad.

## 1832
The *American No. 1* locomotive, with four driving wheels, can manage 100 kph (60 mph).

## 1833
George Stephenson invents the steam-powered brake for slowing trains.

## 1863
The first underground railway is opened in London, England.

## 1869
The Central Pacific and Union Pacific meet at Promontory, Utah, USA, linking the USA's west and east coasts.

## 1879
The first electric locomotive is demonstrated in Germany by Siemens.

## 1891
The Orient Express makes its first run from Paris to Istanbul.

## 1893
The first electrified railway in the USA opens in Baltimore.

## 1897
German engineer Rudolf Diesel demonstrates his diesel engine.

## 1905
The Trans-Siberian Railway is completed.

## 1934
The first successful diesel-electric locomotive is built.

## 1938
The *Mallard* sets the world speed record for a steam locomotive, marking 203 kph (127 mph).

## 1940
The Union Pacific Big Boy locomotives are built in the USA.

## 1990
In France a TGV sets the speed record for an electric train, of 515 kph (322 mph).

## 2001
In Australia the heaviest-ever train (99,732 tonnes) is assembled.

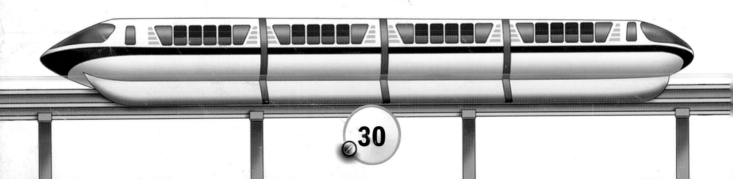

# GLOSSARY

**alternating current**

Electric current that keeps changing direction, flowing one way and then the opposite way.

**bogie**

A frame with four or six wheels.

**carriage**

A railway vehicle for carrying passengers.

**cylinder**

In a steam train, where steam from the boiler makes pistons move in and out.

**diesel locomotive**

A locomotive powered by a diesel engine.

**direct current**

Electric current that flows in the same direction all the time.

**electric locomotive**

A locomotive powered by electricity from an overhead cable or rail.

**firebox**

Where the fuel (coal or wood) is burned in a steam locomotive.

**freight**

Any goods that are carried on a train.

**high-voltage**

Electricity with a large electric force making it flow.

**iron ore**

Rock that the metal iron is extracted from.

**light rail**

A train that runs on tracks through city streets.

**locomotive**

A machine that pulls railway carriages or wagons.

**maglev**

Short for magnetic levitation.

**metro train**

A train that carries lots of passengers and runs from city suburbs or towns into a city.

**monorail**

A railway with one rail instead of two.

**multiple header**

A train pulled by two or more locomotives.

**multiple unit**

A passenger train made up of self-propelled carriages. It has no locomotive.

**piston**

In steam train, the rods that are pushed in and out of cylinders by steam to drive the wheels round.

**signal**

A set of coloured lights on a railway that tells a train driver when to stop or keep going.

**superconductor**

A material that allows electricity to flow through it extremely easily.

**traction motor**

An electric motor that turns the wheels of a locomotive or train.

**valve**

A device that turns on or off the flow of liquid or gas along a pipe.

**wagon**

A railway vehicle for carrying freight.

# INDEX

# WEBFINDER

http://www.railway-technology.com  *Information on the latest trains.*

http://en.wikipedia.org/wiki/Locomotive  *All about different locomotives.*

http://travel.howstuffworks.com/diesel-locomotive.htm  *How a diesel locomotive works.*

http://www.bbc.co.uk/history/games/rocket/rocket.shtml  *Animation of Stephenson's Rocket.*

http://www.bluetrain.co.za  *All about South Africa's luxury Blue Train.*

http://www.steamlocomotive.com/bigboy  *Information and photographs of the biggest steam trains.*

http://www.monorails.org  *All about monorail trains.*

http://www.rtri.or.jp  *Site of the Japanese maglev train.*